In case of loss, please return to:

_____

_____

_____

_____

As a reward: $ _____

RAW HONEST
THE
TOUGH
SAYINGS
OF
JESUS
UNCOMFOR

Michael Kelley

No part of this work may be reproduced or transmitted in any form or by any means, electronic or mechanical, including photocopying and recording, or by any information storage or retrieval system, except as may be expressly permitted in writing by the publisher. Requests for permission should be addressed in writing to LifeWay Press®, One LifeWay Plaza, Nashville, TN 37234-0175

ISBN: 1-4158-5275-8

Dewey Decimal Classification Number: 234.2
Subject Heading: JESUS CHRIST — TEACHINGS \ BELIEF AND DOUBT \ FAITH

Printed in the United States of America

Leadership and Adult Publishing
LifeWay Church Resources
One LifeWay Plaza
Nashville, Tennessee 37234-0175

We believe the Bible has God for its author; salvation for its end; and truth, without any mixture of error, for its matter and that all Scripture is totally true and trustworthy. The 2000 statement of The Baptist Faith and Message is our doctrinal guideline.

Unless otherwise indicated, all Scripture quotations are taken from the Holman Christian Standard Bible® Copyright © 1999, 2000, 2002, 2003 by Holman Bible Publishers. Used by permission. Holman Christian Standard Bible®, Holman CSB®, and HCSB® are federally registered trademarks of Holman Bible Publishers.

Table of Contents

Introduction
"Redefining Jesus?"
Take an honest look at your view of Jesus.

Session 1
"You Have to Give up Everything"
Becoming a Nobody

Session 2
"You People Are Dogs"
Discovering a Faith that Melts Borders

Session 3
"No Forgiveness for You"
Finding the Answer in the Question

Session 4
"I Didn't Come to Bring Peace"
A War That Binds

Meet the Author

Hi, my name is Michael Kelley. I live in Nashville, Tennessee, with my wife, Jana, and my son, Joshua. I grew up in Texas and earned a Master of Divinity at Beeson Divinity School in Birmingham, Alabama. As a writer and teacher, I get the opportunity to speak to students and young adults at conferences and churches across the United States. I also teach at a weekly worship event for young adults in Nashville called Refuge.

I love to be entertained and can be found watching way too much television and way too many movies. I'm not cool enough to listen to music, but I do enjoy all kinds of sports and think that October is the greatest month of the year. I believe that God has put me on this earth to communicate stuff I am experiencing with my community, not stuff that I have already learned and have a firm grasp on. Thanks for walking through these chapters with a fellow journeyer — may you have a bigger picture of Jesus at the end than at the beginning.

Come by and visit me at *www.michaelkelleyonline.com*.

Introduction: Redefining Jesus?

What images come to your mind when you hear or see the name Jesus?

We come from different backgrounds, knowledge bases, and experiences. All those things influence our perceptions, even our perceptions of the same Scriptures we've read about whom Jesus is.

The Bible refers to Jesus as the Alpha and Omega, the Lamb slain before the foundation of the world, and the Savior of the world. In the first chapter of John, He is the Word that was with God, and yet was God, from the beginning. The gospels (Matthew, Mark, Luke, and John) say He is the Son, the Shepherd, and Seeker of the lost. But how do those descriptions play out in our understanding? We may use the same terms, but until we talk it through, we can't be sure if our understanding of those words really mesh.

That's why it's good for us to look at Scripture together. According to the Bible, Jesus has existed throughout history, whether as the mysterious fourth figure in the fiery furnace story of the Old Testament book of Daniel, or as the seemingly blasphemous miracle worker of the New Testament gospels. The image of the person may change, but the essence of who He is remains the same. It is that essence that we will dive into during this study.

THROUGH A NEW LENS

We also see Jesus through different lenses in different seasons of our lives. C.S. Lewis puts great words to this in his Chronicles of Narnia series. The novels present a Christ-figure in the form of a lion named Aslan in a country called Narnia. At one point in the stories, the youngest character, Lucy, returns to Narnia after some time away. She tells Aslan that he is bigger than when she left. Aslan wisely explains that he seems bigger to her, not because he has grown, but because *she* has: "Every year you grow, you will find me bigger." And so it is with our view of Jesus. Our experiences don't change who He is, but they do give us a different vantage point as we, with the guidance of the Holy Spirit, revisit what we understand about Him.

If you grew up going to church, your understanding of Jesus may have been built with macaroni art and felt board stories. The pictures you saw might have portrayed a generous man with a welcoming smile full of love and compassion. We were probably taught that Jesus loved us and wanted to live inside of us. In this way, many of us began our relationship with Him.

For some, though, the relationship stayed within the confines of that scenario. The relationship did not grow as we grew. Our knowledge of Him remained very simple while our lives became increasingly complex. For those of us, it's very possible that this trimmed-down version of the Son of God has been bursting at the seams to escape the small understanding our minds and hearts have created for Him.

It's very possible that this trimmed-down version of the Son of God has been bursting at the seams to escape the small understanding our minds and hearts have created for Him.

THE RULE OF EXPANSION

Relationships are dynamic. They are a give-and-take process as time goes on; years after beginning a relationship with someone, we look back at the early days and wonder if we really knew the person at all back then. Why should our relationship with Christ be any different?

As wonderful as a growing relationship with a living God may sound and seem, there is an uncomfortable element to the continual reformation it requires. As we allow Jesus to burst through the macaroni frame and leap off the felt board, we may not always be comfortable. We may not be so sure we knew Jesus at all back then. Some parts of His ministry may not only be difficult to understand, but downright troubling.

Let's navigate these waters, even if they test our comfort zones. We cannot escape the fact that we don't completely understand everything Jesus said. But, if we are to be in an authentic, growing relationship with Him, we need to explore what we don't understand. Have you avoided certain passages of the Bible because you didn't understand them or they didn't jive with the Jesus you've come to accept? Consider the following: Did Jesus look down on non-Jews? Was He a racist? Did He dishonor His family and ask His followers to do the same? Did Jesus teach about grace through faith, like the rest of the New Testament, or was He more about us proving our love for Him through our actions? These are some of the questions we'll explore in this study.

Hopefully, this experience will help us to face head-on what Scripture teaches — and doesn't teach — about Jesus' life and ministry. If we can revisit what the Bible says, then we can compare what we understand (or misunderstand) the facts to mean. Many of us have staked our faith on Christ. It is up to us, then, to revisit from time to time what we have put our faith in and whether what we've experienced in life has given us a greater ability to understand the truth about Jesus.

THE BEAUTY IN DOUBT

Sometimes an over-simplified view of faith can leave us with the idea that we should shy away from the tough questions out of fear that our faith could be injured. Before we proceed with the study, let's define faith.

In some theological vocabularies, faith is represented as "the absence of doubt." With that definition, the measure of how much faith we have is determined by how little doubt accompanies it.

But is there really anything in our lives that doesn't contain a certain measure of doubt or at least questioning? Unfortunately, an over-simplified definition of faith doesn't leave room for questions, and so we end up living with closeted doubt that only shows its face during the most grim and troubling times in our lives.

There is a more realistic — and more authentic — way to approach faith and doubt. Our definition of faith should be more than the absence of doubt; instead, doubt can be an essential element to the process of faith. We have faith in something bigger than our doubts and questions. We don't have to fear them. If we can push hard into our questions instead of hiding them, we trust God to be bigger. And He is. God is big enough to receive us, doubt and all. Doubts and questions do not counter faith; instead, they should push us deeper.

Let's embrace authentic faith. Let's look at all that we know about Christ, even the parts we can't completely figure out. Let's let Him speak to us through what the Bible teaches, even if we don't completely understand. Even when, as in the Scripture for Session 1, it seems He tells a self-righteous young man that the key to salvation is not faith at all — but works ...

Listen to the audio file "Conflict Insulation." It will come via email from your group leader. Think about the following questions as you listen and come to your group's first study lesson ready to discuss your thoughts.

• How does our avoidance of conflict relate to our faith?
• How do we try to insulate our faith in a "comfortable fortress of security?"
• How does navigating through doubt actually strengthen your faith?

"You Have to Give up Everything"

I love the salad bar. Not the salad, per se, but the salad bar as a whole. There is a huge difference between the two. The salad is green, leafy, and distasteful. That's why I love the bar. Cheese, bacon, eggs, tomatoes, dressing, ham — all of these things make the salad bearable. Unfortunately, the salad bar dilutes the nutritional value of what is underneath. You have to ask the question: With all that stuff piled on the top, can you really call what is on your plate a salad any more?

Perhaps, in the church, we have bellied up to the salad bar in terms of the gospel. We have piled stuff on top of the good news, rendering the gospel much less nutritious than it once was, and maybe even making us wonder: Is this really the gospel at all?

To return to the healthy, trimmed down version of the gospel, where else would we turn except to Jesus Himself? So what does this "salad master" say to someone who asks the simplest of questions about the nature of this good news? The answer might surprise you …

"He said to Him, 'Teacher, I have kept all these from my youth.'

"Then, looking at him, Jesus loved him and said to him, 'You lack one thing: Go, sell all you have and give to the poor, and you will have treasure in heaven. Then come, follow Me.' But he was stunned at this demand, and he went away grieving, because he had many possessions.

"Jesus looked around and said to His disciples, 'How hard it is for those who have wealth to enter the kingdom of God!' But the disciples were astonished at His words. Again Jesus said to them, 'Children, how hard it is to enter the kingdom of God! It is easier for a camel to go through the eye of a needle than for a rich person to enter the kingdom of God.'

"So they were even more astonished, saying to one another, 'Then who can be saved?'" (Mark 10:20-26).

"You Have to Give up Everything"

BECOMING A NOBODY ...

IS FAITH ABOUT WORKS?

Our Christian subculture is not short on methodology. We have methods for discipleship, Bible study, evangelism, and more.

> Think through the different evangelism methods you have been exposed to. Which, if any, of the methods did you find to be effective? What about the experiences made you uncomfortable?

Traditional methods offer an easy-to-understand process. Sometimes, however, they may be too easy. At times, it seems all anyone has to do to step into faith is memorize a few verses and pray a scripted prayer.

Was that Jesus' method? We would expect our methods would be built on His life. If so, then Mark 10 gives us something to think about.

Take a few moments to read through the account that has become known as the story of the rich, young ruler. Though there are parallel versions in Matthew 19 and Luke 18, the account in Mark 10:17-31 is the most detailed:

"As He was setting out on a journey, a man ran up, knelt down before Him, and asked Him, 'Good Teacher, what must I do to inherit eternal life?'
'Why do you call Me good?' Jesus asked him. 'No one is good but One—God. You know the commandments:
  Do not murder;
  do not commit adultery;
  do not steal;
  do not bear false witness;
  do not defraud;
  honor your father and mother.'

"He said to Him, 'Teacher, I have kept all these from my youth.'

"Then, looking at him, Jesus loved him and said to him, 'You lack one thing: Go, sell all you have and give to the poor, and you will have treasure in heaven. Then come, follow Me.' But he was stunned at this demand, and he went away grieving, because he had many possessions.

"Jesus looked around and said to His disciples, 'How hard it is for those who have wealth to enter the kingdom of God!' But the disciples were astonished at His words. Again Jesus said to them, 'Children, how hard it is to enter the kingdom of God! It is easier for a camel to go through the eye of a needle than for a rich person to enter the kingdom of God.'

"So they were even more astonished, saying to one another, 'Then who can be saved?'

"Looking at them, Jesus said, 'With men it is impossible, but not with God, because all things are possible with God.'

"Peter began to tell Him, 'Look, we have left everything and followed You.'
'I assure you,' Jesus said, 'there is no one who has left house, brothers or sisters, mother or father, children, or fields because of Me and the gospel, who will not receive 100 times more, now at this time — houses, brothers and sisters, mothers and children, and fields, with persecutions — and eternal life in the age to come. But many who are first will be last, and the last first'" (Mark 10:17-31).

Listen to the audio file "Conflict Insulation." Your group leader will send it via e-mail. Begin to think about how navigating through doubt can actually strengthen your faith.

At first glance, Jesus found Himself in an evangelistic dream-come-true. Even without a prompt of a clever spiritual opening statement or Christian T-shirt, a man came to Jesus and asked: "What do I have to do to have eternal life?"

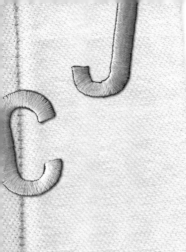

Some would think Jesus should have been licking His chops because this man was primed and ready. They would say that all that was left was for Jesus to hand him a tract and lead him through the sinner's prayer. From the perspective of that kind of hard-line, prowling-for-converts way of thinking, Jesus' response is baffling. He seemed to make it harder rather than easier on the guy.

But even from what you might call a more process-oriented point of view, Jesus' response makes us ponder. From the whole of the New Testament, we know salvation to be a product of faith and grace as opposed to simply us doing good things to earn God's love. In light of that, you would think Jesus would have said, "Frankly, sir, your question is flawed. There is, in fact, *nothing* at all you can *do* to inherit eternal life; the issue at hand is not your works, be they good or bad; the issue is one of faith. Do not *do*; but *believe*."

But Jesus didn't respond that way. He didn't even mention faith. In fact, He seemed to do the opposite. In essence, Jesus said, "Perhaps you have not done enough! *Do this one more thing*, and then you can have eternal life."

Have you ever had the sense there was always *just one more thing* to do to get the "spiritual life thing" right?

In your theology, what is the relationship between what you believe and what you do?

WHO WAS THIS RICH, YOUNG RULER?

Let's build a mental picture of this scene:

Jesus drew a crowd everywhere He went. Because He was known to be a miracle worker, a feeder of multitudes, and a compassionate teacher, He attracted the kinds of people that really *needed* something — food, healing, understanding, or any other escape from their desperation. The people who were crowding around Jesus were probably the poor, the sick, and the sinners.

Then, along came someone different. In the Matthew account, this man is called young. Luke makes it clear that he is a ruler of some kind. As was common in the first century, he probably dressed the part. So, we reasonably imagine that a man dressed like a ruler ran into a crowd of destitute people.

Yes, he *ran*. Running would have been undignified for anyone in that culture, much less someone with a great deal of authority. Apparently, whatever this man was feeling made him desperate enough to throw his respectability at Jesus' feet. Then the scene took one more step toward bizarre. This man — obviously an important and well known community figure — who had already humiliated himself in front of a crowd of common people asked Jesus a question: What do I need to do to have eternal life?

> What kind of profile would you build on this guy based on his question? How do you imagine the situation played out?

Two facts jump out from the man's question. First of all, he called Jesus "good." He used the term for *good* in his language that means intrinsically good — it was a word not used lightly. In fact, in that culture, no one was ever called this kind of *good* except God Himself. Clearly, the man had come to some conclusions about who Jesus was.

Secondly, the man was at the end of his rope. Image to the wind, kneeling

there in the dust, he looked up at Jesus and asked, "What must I do to inherit eternal life?" This question was strange coming from him because he should have known the Jewish answer to that question: "Obey the law of God!"

Considering all this, you have to wonder if this rich, young ruler has gotten an unfairly negative reputation through the years. Maybe he was not some spoiled, haughty, know-it-all who was proud of his righteousness. Instead, he seems more like a disillusioned church kid who knew all the "right" answers. He had done all the right things, but they had not fulfilled him. Perhaps, this is a picture of a legalist at the end of his rope, asking some bottom-line questions: "Is there something more to pleasing God than just keeping the rules? Is there something deeper than the law? What am I missing?"

At first response, Jesus did tell him to keep the law. Then, He even went a step further. If this guy had indeed kept all those laws, then there was one thing that he hadn't done: he hadn't sold everything he owned and given it to the poor. Why didn't Jesus dispel the man's doubts and offer a word of comfort about faith and grace instead of giving him one more thing to *do?*

REDEFINING BLESSING

If we are surprised by Jesus' response, we are not alone. Notice the reaction of the disciples. The passage says — *two* times — that they were amazed.

Why would the disciples be surprised at Jesus' response?

As for the disciples, perhaps their amazement came from their ideas of what it meant to be blessed by God. Think for a moment about the fabulous lives celebrities live today. You can turn on any entertainment TV channel and hear about how good it is to be someone rich and famous. The first century disciples of Jesus would look at these kinds of fabulous lives and say simply, "P. Diddy is blessed. J. Lo is blessed. Britney is blessed."

To that first century Jew, if people were wealthy, if they were healthy, if they had many children and also many goats, then clearly they were blessed. On the other hand, if they were sick or poor, then God was cursing them because of their behavior.

When we understand that, we can see a reason the disciples would be so flabbergasted at the words of Jesus — He was telling this man to rid himself of the very things that, in his culture, evidenced God's blessing in his life. It would have made more sense to first century ears for Jesus to say, "Blessed are the rich. Blessed are the healthy. Blessed are the comfortable." Jesus, of course, flipped that idea upside down. Into this culture defined by material blessing, He said things like: "Blessed are the poor. Blessed are those who mourn. Blessed are the hungry and thirsty. Give away all you have."

What about you? How do you define blessing?
What blessings are in your life?

In your own words, how would you describe Jesus' definition of blessing?

Does our culture's idea of blessing still have some materialism wound up in

it? Perhaps that makes us uncomfortable with the requirement Jesus placed on the young ruler. We could still have the tendency to look at God with a works/rewards kind of attitude, meaning that when we are living rightly, then He will give us more and more stuff. Therefore, if we have been given more and more stuff, then we know we have been living rightly.

GRACE EXPECTATIONS

There is, however, another reason that I am shocked by Jesus' response. I tend to want Jesus to say, "What must you *do?* See, that's just your problem. It's not about doing — it's about receiving. So stop trying and just have faith." It seems to me that if there was ever a time to talk about faith, this was it. Instead, Jesus gives this desperate man something else to accomplish — and it's a really hard thing. That goes against what I've come to believe about grace.

If that really is what Jesus is doing — putting one more thing on this man's spiritual back — this Jesus doesn't seem very sympathetic, does He? This man came in desperation and humility. He made himself look ridiculous in front of the crowd. All that, and he had already lived a good life. He wasn't a tax collector or a prostitute. He was a righteous man. Yet, throughout all of his rule-keeping, he found something missing. And Jesus responded by giving him one more thing to do?

THE HIDDEN KEY

Tucked away in this passage is an all-important detail:

"Then, looking at him, Jesus loved him and said to him, 'You lack one thing: Go, sell all you have and give to the poor, and you will have treasure in heaven. Then come, follow Me,'" (Mark 10:21).

Jesus looked at the man and loved him. He loved him in his desperation. He loved him before he did anything. Jesus loved the man before he refused the command to do more. The love of God wasn't dependent on what the man did.

Do you believe Jesus loves you even before you follow Him?
Do you ever feel He is judging your performance — that He'll love you more if you do better?

When you are well connected to Jesus' love, how is your life affected?

How would you describe a person who lives consistently in the truth that Jesus' love for them precedes anything they might do to earn it?

The legalist in us reverses the order. We live like the passage says that Jesus told him to go sell everything he owned, and then, after he hypothetically did it, Jesus looked at him and loved him. When we put love at the end rather than the beginning, we can wind up bitter and frustrated over what we have to give up in our Christian lives. We live an unadmittedly jaded existence in an endless effort to prove ourselves to God, to earn His approval.

Listen to "The Rich Young Ruler" by Derek Webb. What do the lyrics say about our society?

In what ways do you feel you have to prove yourself to God?

Do you maintain other relationships in your life in which you feel like you always have to justify that you deserve to be in the relationship? How would you describe God's perspective on that kind of relationship?

But since the command comes after the love, regardless of what the command is, the only option for us is to believe that the command of Christ is made *out* of that love.

IDENTITY CHECK

Consider for a moment how we define ourselves. Think back to some "first conversation" you had with someone recently. After a cordial introduction of names, usually the next question sounds something like, "So what do you do? Where are you from?" These are inquiries into who a person is, and rightly so, because we define ourselves by the answers to those questions. Our identity is wound up in what we do, how we live, and what we have.

What are the first three things you usually tell people about yourself?

How important is your career or your achievements to your identity?

How many of your friends would you say *really* know who you are (instead of just knowing facts about you)?

How well do *you* feel like you really know who you are?

It seems the traditional identity marks of our society are declining. In generations past, people could define themselves by their careers, their family names, or their educations. But now, those marks are crumbling. People change careers throughout their lives. Families take different shapes in different seasons. Most of us don't even have the same name as both of our parents. We are a generation unable to easily define ourselves to our peers and even to ourselves. We are left asking, "Who am I? What are the markers that define me?"

Here's the point: *This is the question that Jesus was trying to get the young man to ask.* The man knew how people defined him. People defined him the same way we define him today — as rich, as young, and as a ruler. Jesus wanted more. He wanted to get to this man's core, to his real self. Selling his possessions, even considering it, would strip this man of his marks of identity. Only by stripping those things away, in that moment of crisis, could he define himself the way Jesus wanted — by whom his faith was in.

The question of identity can really only be answered in a moment of crisis. In other words, it can really only be answered when something attached to your core is taken out of your control: health, achievements, career, family life, and so forth. Who are you when those things are altered or threatened? Who would the rich young ruler be if he sold his possessions? He would not be rich or a ruler; he would have nothing external left to offer — no money, no works, no prestige — just himself.

PREVIOUSLY IN JUDEA ...
This is what Jesus was moving toward. How do we know? Our biggest clue is hidden a few verses back, before this story began. It's in the conversation Jesus had with his disciples back in Mark 10:13.

"Some people were bringing little children to Him so He might touch them, but His disciples rebuked them. When Jesus saw it, He was indignant and said to them, 'Let the little children come to Me. Don't stop them, for the kingdom of God belongs to such as these. I assure you: Whoever does not welcome the kingdom of God like a little child will never enter it.' After taking them in His arms, He laid His hands on them and blessed them," (Mark 10:13-16).

Though it's impossible to know the disciples' exact motivation, we can make a good historical guess. In that society, children were not real people; they had nothing to offer mainstream culture. As a general rule, they were expected to simply live in preparation for how they could contribute to the family. In what was a shocking move, Jesus claimed that the kingdom of God

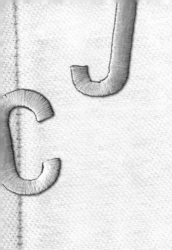

belonged to these very children the disciples saw simply as an annoyance. To Jesus, these nobodies had a quality that was not only kingdom-worthy, it had escaped the richest, the most righteous, and the most productive members of society.

In light of this, it follows that Jesus would draw the rich young ruler into this quality of nothingness in order to embrace God's true kingdom. But, the only way for the man to get there was by getting rid of what had previously given him significance.

Actually, this is what Jesus wants from all of us — to be nobodies! Nobodies cannot come to God offering their contributions. Nobodies cannot tell God who they are. Nobodies have no claim on their lives. Nobodies do not rely on trivial marks of identity; their significance comes from something deeper. They find their meaning in the life and identity in Jesus.

For the rich young ruler, that proved impossible. He could not embrace an existence in which he had nothing to bring to the table. He could not stomach the crisis of nothingness; so he missed the true blessing of having Jesus offer him significance in something deeper than his job or title.

Can you hear the voice of Jesus from the pages of Scripture? Can you feel His hands trying to pry your clenched fists from whatever is keeping you from true poverty and thus, true wealth? Listen to Him as he calls out .

> "Go, sell your self-righteousness."
> "Go, sell your dreams of fame and fortune."
> "Go, sell your popularity."
> "Go, sell your efforts to secure a comfortable future for yourself."
> "Come, and trust me, for I love you."

Do we define ourselves as Jesus defines us, or by the way we have traditionally defined ourselves? We, too, need to trade in those marks of identity.

Are you living a life defined by Jesus? If not, what is your life defined by?

Take a moment to honestly reflect. Is there anything — possession or perspective — you need to trade off so that you can approach Christ in true faith?

Processing ....

☐ Engage your community in a discussion of this question: "What defines you?"

☐ To experience a visual illustration of spiritual poverty, intentionally drive through a downtown area on your commute.

☐ As an exercise in "becoming poor," take no money with you for an entire day. Journal your experiences.

☐ Spend some time re-examining exactly what you would call "the gospel."

Notes

Notes

"You People Are Dogs"

You can probably find a picture of Jesus in the basement of your church. In it, He may have long, flowing hair, a neatly trimmed beard, lily white skin, face turned up toward heaven, welcoming blue eyes, and a heavenly light coming from above giving Him a bright, shining complexion. It's the kind of Jesus that looks like He wants nothing more than to be your best friend.

Nice picture, but it's a poor sense of reality. I doubt there was a glowing orb that followed Jesus wherever He went. I don't think He walked around with His eyes turned upward. And I sure don't think He had skin that white. The reality is that He was a very ordinary looking Middle Eastern man. He had no physical attributes that would distinguish Him from anyone else — just another tradesman from a poor family.

At least the welcoming expression that reminds us He wants to be our best friend is right.

Right?

"He replied, 'I was sent only to the lost sheep of the house of Israel.'

"But she came, knelt before Him, and said, 'Lord, help me!'

"He answered, 'It isn't right to take the children's bread and throw it to their dogs.'

"'Yes, Lord,' she said, 'yet even the dogs eat the crumbs that fall from their masters' table!'" (Matthew 15:24-27).

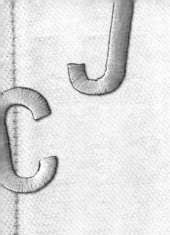

"You People Are Dogs"

DISCOVERING A FAITH THAT MELTS BORDERS

"When Jesus left there, He withdrew to the area of Tyre and Sidon. Just then a Canaanite woman from that region came and kept crying out, 'Have mercy on me, Lord, Son of David! My daughter is cruelly tormented by a demon.'
Yet He did not say a word to her. So His disciples approached Him and urged Him, 'Send her away because she cries out after us.'

"He replied, 'I was sent only to the lost sheep of the house of Israel.'
But she came, knelt before Him, and said, 'Lord, help me!'

"He answered, 'It isn't right to take the children's bread and throw it to their dogs.'
'Yes, Lord,' she said, 'yet even the dogs eat the crumbs that fall from their masters' table!'

"Then Jesus replied to her, 'Woman, your faith is great. Let it be done for you as you want.' And from that moment her daughter was cured" (Matthew 15:21-28).

There are some things that just look better on paper. We may like the idea of them, but they don't translate well into reality.

For me, sushi is one of those things. I enjoy the idea of having a sophisticated palate. I like the concept of a healthy way to enjoy food in its most natural state. The practical problem is simply the taste. In the end, no matter how good the idea is, it still tastes like raw fish and seaweed to me.

As for the "looks good on paper" problem, sometimes I think the same thing about what we Christians call "unity." We champion the cause of unity and love the idea. We talk about it and study it. Every Christ-follower intellectually assents to the need for unity in the body of Christ. Yet, in most urban areas, there are literally hundreds of churches — many facing each other across the intersection.

Some are separated by different nuances of belief or practice. There's worship style, for instance: the regular worshipers, the charismatic worshipers, the liturgists, the readers, the silent, and those who believe in it all. I'm afraid churches separated by style preferences are, in many cases, little more than gatherings of cliques each devoted to its own members.

Then, unbelievably after all the decades that have passed, there are still churches separated by race. For the most part, these fellowships have completely unrelated existences. While there is nothing wrong with recognizing cultural distinctions, particularly where language barriers are concerned, all the different church labels along the road have to make us wonder how far we've really come on being the unified church in the world.

If there is anyone who has ever walked on the earth that we would consider to be open to relationships, it is Jesus Christ. He consistently associated with people who most would consider off limits. However, in looking at the body of Christ in the 21st century, the same spirit doesn't always exist.

How would you describe your racial biases and their sources?

The church of Jesus Christ has only one great mission. That mission is simply to continue Jesus' work and spread His story. Jesus didn't leave instructions about church structure or worship when He gave His final words to His followers. He did not hand down edicts about living righteous lives or even loving others. His last words were ones of *mission*.

Take a look at Matthew 28 and remember Jesus' final command to His followers:

"'Go, therefore, and make disciples of all nations, baptizing them in the name of the Father and of the Son and of the Holy Spirit, teaching them to observe everything I have commanded you. And remember, I am with you always, to the end of the age'" (Matthew 28:19-20).

He said to "go," or more correctly, Jesus actually used a verb tense that meant "as you are going." He assumed that His followers would be going, and as they were, they should be making disciples. He said they should keep going and making disciples until every part of the earth has heard the story.

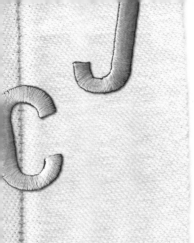

How do you view sharing the gospel as you go? What does it look like in your life??

Jesus' last command presented the gospel outside of cultural boundaries. In fact, His whole point was to scale cultural walls. His story is one that was meant to transcend boundaries set up by nations and people groups. Though the people of God might look different in different places, the message of God is supposed to be planted in every soil on the planet. Jesus began it, and He expected it to continue.

Because most of us have our own understanding of the mission Christ gave the church, we have very specific expectations of how Christians should act. As we remember back through the story of Jesus, we have certain expectations of how He would have responded in all situations.

Then comes Matthew 15:21-28, an account that makes us shake our heads a bit and think, *Did I read that right?* In this chapter, Jesus responds in a way that is, at the least, surprising and to some may seem intolerable.

"When Jesus left there, He withdrew to the area of Tyre and Sidon. Just then a Canaanite woman from that region came and kept crying out, 'Have mercy on me, Lord, Son of David! My daughter is cruelly tormented by a demon.'

"Yet He did not say a word to her. So His disciples approached Him and urged Him, 'Send her away because she cries out after us.'

"He replied, 'I was sent only to the lost sheep of the house of Israel.'

"But she came, knelt before Him, and said, 'Lord, help me!'

"He answered, 'It isn't right to take the children's bread and throw it to their dogs.'
'Yes, Lord,' she said, 'yet even the dogs eat the crumbs that fall from their masters' table!'

"Then Jesus replied to her, 'Woman, your faith is great. Let it be done for you as you want.' And from that moment her daughter was cured" (Matthew 15:21-28).

Session 2 – *You People Are Dogs*

In all honesty, most of us would have to acknowledge a certain amount of racial bias within ourselves. Be it from ignorance, personal experience with a small number of people, or regional upbringing, most of us carry some kind of presupposition about other people groups that we know we need to overcome. But this story doesn't seem to inspire us to do that, does it? Let's look closer and see.

THOSE KIND OF PEOPLE

Before we interpret this account to support racial bias as an accepted way of life, let's look at who this woman and her people were.

Jesus had purposely withdrawn to the region of Tyre and Sidon (two non-Jewish cities). These cities in northwest Philistia were frequently referred to in the Old Testament as symbols of paganism and godlessness; in fact, they were specifically condemned by Isaiah, Jeremiah, and Ezekiel. According to these Old Testament prophets Tyre and Sidon were poster children for the righteous judgment and anger of God.

> What do you know about the typical Jewish opinion regarding the Gentiles?

> How do you think the disciples felt about being in this region? What relationship between people groups in contemporary culture reflects the prejudice between the Jews and Gentiles?

Throughout the history of the Jews, their identity was their special calling from God to believe only in Him and to be blessed as His nation. They were to proactively set themselves apart from people groups who didn't acknowledge God as the one true God. Because of this understanding, the

This Cannanite woman belonged to Northwest Phoenician cities — founded long before the Israelites inherited Canaan. This area became known as a center for trade. In 870 B.C., Ahab married Jezebel, the daughter of a Phoenician king, bringing Baal worship to Israel. Ezekiel describes one king from this region as the epitome of pride.

Gentile

To the Jewish people, the word *Gentile* became synonymous with *pagan* and *heathen*. From the time God made Israel a holy nation (Exodus. 19:6), it was clear that no other nation had such laws or such a God. When Israel was persecuted, tension heightened between herself and the outside nations, causing the Psalmist to curse the nations (PS. 9, 59, 137). This might explain the disciples' scorn for an outsider trying to take advantage of Jesus. Despite Israel's distinct anointing from God, it's clear that other nations have the ability to worship God (1 Kings 8:41-43; Isa. 49:6).

Jews distanced themselves from everyone who wasn't Jewish. Non-Jews were referred to as Gentiles. Since Tyre and Sidon were not only Gentile towns but also had a reputation for great wickedness, a Jewish person of that day would have felt free to disregard, if not have contempt for, the citizens there. They would have almost seen it as their spiritual responsibility to create as much social distance as possible.

BEAUTIFUL DESPERATION

In Matthew 15, the woman approaching Jesus and His followers was representative of the people who the Jews had regarded with contempt for centuries. The disciples would have known clearly that her national history was filled with rebellion and wickedness, and she would have been considered radically unclean by them. Just knowing all that — and remembering that she knew all that as well — reveals something special about this particular Gentile woman who was willing to approach Jesus.

First of all, she demonstrated that she knew something of how to approach God, because she was clearly familiar with Judaism. She used a very Jewish title for Jesus, calling him Son of David. Not only did she demonstrate her knowledge, but she also demonstrated her passion. The description of her cries were not only loud, but the wording implies that they had been going on a while. She was in passionate and desperate need and was doing her best to approach Jesus with the utmost respect despite the upturned noses of the disciples.

She actually seems like the ideal person for Jesus to help. She believed He could help, she approached Him in the proper way, and she was passionate about her situation. She exhibited all of the classic attributes that we think of as "keys" to getting a response from God; if there is one, she was exhibiting the perfect formula of humility and faith. So surely Jesus would help her — right?

So how did Jesus respond to one so desperate and yet so respectful of Him? He first responded by ignoring her, which seemed to suit the disciples. They were uncomfortable not only because of the wailing but because this was a Gentile woman, a pagan, something below them, unclean. The disciples jumped on board at the thought that Jesus was just as disgusted with her as they were. They urged Him to send her away, so Jesus responded by telling the woman in essence, "I'd really love to help, but the fact is that I was sent to Israel." The disciples may have caught each other's eyes or snickered to themselves, but the woman would not take no for an answer. Instead, she threw herself in front of the procession and continued to wail, "Help me!"

Session 2 - *You People Are Dogs*

Since ignoring her hadn't worked, Jesus made a subtle statement about her status: "I can't take the children's bread and give it to the dogs." In other words: "I can't take the goodness that is reserved for the chosen people of God and give it to someone like you." The disciples must have loved watching Jesus put this woman in her place. Keep in mind that dogs were not very commonly kept as pets in that day. They were scavengers. They were filthy, and they were dangerous. So not only did Jesus ignore the woman, He also dramatically insulted her.

But, this determined woman didn't seem to bat an eye. In essence, she said to Jesus, "You're right. I know what your people think of me. But I am asking You to have pity even on a dog like me."

Who could have seen it coming? Jesus was pleased with her response. In fact, He was pleased enough to heal her daughter immediately.

> What do you think pleased Jesus in the woman's response?
> What did her words reveal about her faith?

PURITY: INSIDE OUT

Let's explore what happened between Jesus and this Gentile woman. There was something there besides residual racial and cultural tension. On the surface, it seemed that Jesus was agreeing with His cultures' assessment of this annoying woman. If we look a little deeper though, we see another issue at the heart of His seemingly harsh response. As usual, Jesus didn't mind using shocking — and effective — ways to make His point.

Let's scroll back a bit and consider what had happened with Jesus and His followers just before this encounter with the Gentile woman. When we look back to Matthew 15:1-20, Jesus was facing off with the Pharisees on the issue of cleanliness — a hot topic in the Jewish religious system.

"Then Pharisees and scribes came from Jerusalem to Jesus and asked, 'Why do Your disciples break the tradition of the elders? For they don't wash their hands when they eat!'

"He answered them, 'And why do you break God's commandment because of your tradition? For God said:

Honor your father and your mother; and,
The one who speaks evil of father or mother
must be put to death.

"But you say, "Whoever tells his father or mother, 'Whatever benefit you might have received from me is a gift [committed to the temple]'—he does not have to honor his father." In this way, you have revoked God's word because of your tradition. Hypocrites! Isaiah prophesied correctly about you when he said:

These people honor Me with their lips,
but their heart is far from Me.
They worship Me in vain,
teaching as doctrines the commands of men.'"

"Summoning the crowd, He told them, 'Listen and understand: It's not what goes into the mouth that defiles a man, but what comes out of the mouth, this defiles a man.' Then the disciples came up and told Him, 'Do You know that the Pharisees took offense when they heard this statement?' He replied, 'Every plant that My heavenly Father didn't plant will be uprooted. Leave them alone! They are blind guides. And if the blind guide the blind, both will fall into a pit.' Then Peter replied to Him, 'Explain this parable to us.' 'Are even you still lacking in understanding?' He asked. 'Don't you realize that whatever goes into the mouth passes into the stomach and is eliminated? But what comes out of the mouth comes from the heart, and this defiles a man. For from the heart come evil thoughts, murders, adulteries, sexual immoralities, thefts, false testimonies, blasphemies. These are the things that defile a man, but eating with unwashed hands does not defile a man'" (Matthew 15:1-20).

The Pharisees had found yet one more criticism of Jesus' ministry. It came from a simple omission by Jesus' disciples — they didn't regularly wash their hands before they ate. In not doing this, the disciples made themselves unclean according to Jewish tradition. Jesus was quick to defend His disciples, claiming that their omission didn't have anything to do with real purity. Real, spiritual purity, according to Jesus, was an internal matter rather than an external one.

While Jesus' statement may seem essential to us, He was treading on thin ice with the religious thinking of His day. When He explained His perspective to the Pharisees, they got angry and walked away. He explained it further to the disciples with a word picture, but they missed His point. Everyone around

Him seemed unable to grasp that, fundamentally, purity is about the heart. It is not about what you eat or do not eat. It is not about whether you wash or do not wash. In fact, it is not even about where you live or do not live. It is not about what race you are — or are not.

It was on the heels of this conversation about purity that Jesus withdrew to Tyre and Sidon. In traveling to the Gentile countryside, Jesus was after more than fresh air; He wanted to make a comment about the real nature of purity in a real life kind of way. Is it possible that this encounter with the woman, at some level, served to teach the disciples a lesson about real purity? What better place to explain purity than the most unclean place they could have imagined?

How do you define purity?

How do you differentiate between inner and outer purity?

Listen to the audio file "Fireworks!" It will come via e-mail from your group leader. Then think about why you think God puts us in situations where we have absolutely no control.

What is the most unclean place you know?

No doubt the disciples were uncomfortable being in Gentile cities. To them, the whole environment would have felt dirty. Jesus, however, was looking for something. When He heard the cries, "Son of David, have mercy on me!" He must have known that He had found what He was looking for. This woman in need would help Him show His disciples just what being clean is all about.

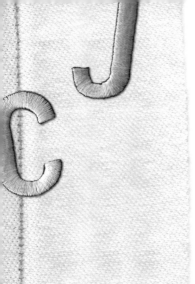

The situation set up perfectly. Every layer of the interaction *seemed* to support the typical Jewish perspective on the Gentiles. And the woman seemed to play along. Rather than respond to Jesus with contempt, she simply expressed her great need: "I might as well be a dog, because that is how much I need you to work in my life. I need you. I need you. I need you. Help me, please." That is precisely the response Jesus wanted. Her expression of need is the ideal picture of true purity.

Think about that. If this woman's response is our picture of purity, then we may have to drastically change some of our own ideas. Right now, we look at statements like those in the Sermon on the Mount (Matthew 5) where Jesus says, "Blessed are the pure in heart for they will see God," and we think that our job is to try our best to clean ourselves up. We busily examine every single one of our motives, making sure that we not only say the right thing but say it with the right motive behind it.

But, when Jesus wanted to illustrate real purity, He did not choose a woman commended for her moral perfection; He chose one who knew how much she needed Him. In that dirty place, Jesus found something clean. What could be clean about her being willing to be called a dog? *Desperation.* Desperate situations make for pure people, because in that desperate moment, those people see their need most clearly.

NEED OF HIM

This desperate woman wasn't thinking about her motives. She wasn't thinking about how foolish she looked. She wasn't thinking about the judgmental glances from those around her. She was thinking about one thing: her need for Jesus. Isn't that what real purity is? Is it not single-mindedness? Is it not whole-heartedness? Is it not complete dedication? *That* is purity — not necessarily the complete absence of the immoral. Jesus saw the purity of desperation in this woman — the very thing the Pharisees and even His own disciples lacked.

Those who do not know their need are very proud of their accomplish ments. Their hearts are divided. However, those who know they have nothing before the Lord come in purity because they know they are needy. What we see in this woman — this unclean, "second rate" Gentile woman — is purity.

Not only is she a lesson in purity, she is a lesson in faith, and maybe those two attributes are linked more closely than we realize. Remember why Jesus commended this woman: He didn't say, "Woman, you have great purity!" He said, "Woman, you have great faith!" He said this because when we express our need for God, we say something about Him. It's no small matter to be in need — not when our whole society frowns upon the idea of being in need and asking for help. When we are willing to come to God with nothing in our hands, nothing to show Him, in the purity of desperation, what we say with our actions is that He is the great provider. We lift Him up as the need-meeter. After all, that is why we come to Him.

When we come in need, we lower ourselves and exalt Him by saying, "There are not many relationships in my life where I can express my need. People will judge me, look down on me, or think me weak. I am coming to You, Father, and in so doing, I am making a statement that I believe that you are good and powerful. I am stating once and for all that I exalt you as the source of all that I need." That takes great faith.

Listen to "Changed" by Phil Joel. What specific things has God changed about you?

In a culture of abundance, of relative economic stability and suburbia, of 401K's and insurance policies, we have to wonder: are we ever really conscious of our need? Our desperation? If not, do we ever approach Jesus whole-heartedly? Without being cognisant of our need, do we ever come in purity?

> In what ways do you feel comfortable (or not) talking about your own needs that drive you to God?

Processing ...

☐ Visit a church associated with a different ethnicity with your Bible study group.

☐ Spend some time journaling about how you view the concept of purity.

☐ Take a walk through a place you would consider "unclean."

Notes

Notes

"No Forgiveness for You"

Why does my 2-year-old want to push the limits? He is discovering the boundaries in his life that separate what he can get away with and what he can't. More times than not, when he discovers a boundary, he doesn't want to avoid it; he wants to be as close to it as possible. He knows he can't walk in the street, so he likes to tiptoe on the edge of the sidewalk. He knows he can't put his finger in his nose, so he likes to put it right beside his nose instead.

I guess most of us are like that, though. We always seem to want to walk right up to the line that moves us from acceptable to unacceptable behavior, even though we know there are consequences for crossing that line. We do it in friendships, in dating relationships, and in our relationship with God. In most of those relationships, if you cross that line too many times, you put the relationship in serious jeopardy.

But amazingly, that is not so with God. You cannot out sin His grace. You cannot disobey enough to warrant His rejection. At least I don't think you can …

"Anyone who is not with Me is against Me, and anyone who does not gather with Me scatters. Because of this, I tell you, people will be forgiven every sin and blasphemy, but the blasphemy against the Spirit will not be forgiven" (Matthew 12:30-31).

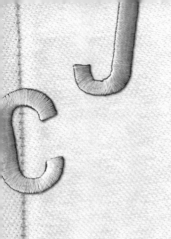

"No Forgiveness for You"

FINDING THE ANSWER IN THE QUESTION

RULES

We like having some rules, don't we? They give us security. We know what to expect — and what not to. They mean there are fewer surprises to throw us off. If someone refuses to follow the rules, the result is insecurity, fear, distrust. This becomes ever more clear as we look at the world's current fascination with reality television.

In the beginning, the rules for reality TV were clear. On some programs, contestants had to form strategic alliances with phrases like, "I give you my word," or, "You can count on me," or, "We have a handshake agreement." But, an unspoken rule on those shows was that contestants could choose which of those alliances to break.

On other shows, desperate women clamored over a moderately handsome and morally despicable guy. At the end of each episode was an elaborate ceremony where he feigned affection and regret that any of the women had to go home. Nevertheless, he made the choice, offering a rose to those who stayed and nothing to the losers. Those were the rules.

But the most recent trend has to do with broken rules and unexpected twists. For example, the reality dating shows include a new format with an element of danger: the sudden death, one-on-one date. At the end of each one-on-one date, the guy had the option of giving out a rose or sending the bachelorette home *right then*. Those twists stunned contestants — and audiences.

The rules had changed! This was not what they had expected or signed up for. After these kinds of twists, levels of distrust, hatred, and insecurity rose. Should we be surprised? That's what happens when a person thinks they have a firm grasp on a situation and the rules change without warning.

The same can be true of our relationship with God.

How do rules meet needs inside of us?

What are some of the rules (your expectations)
in your relationship with God?

WHAT ARE THE RULES?

Matthew 12 has one of those verses that can feel an awful lot like a serious
plot twist — seemingly in the words of Christ Himself.

If asked, most of us would say you simply cannot out-sin the grace of God
— we would call that a hard and fast rule. There is nothing you could do that
God would not forgive. Even if you lived a prodigal life in constant and willful
rebellion for years, you could always come back to a father that runs to meet
you on the road home. But we come to Matthew 12:31, and that rule seems
to not apply.

**"Because of this, I tell you, people will be forgiven every sin and blasphemy, but
the blasphemy against the Spirit will not be forgiven," (Matthew 12:31).**

How do you interpret what Jesus is saying here?

What is this unforgivable sin described here?
Why is it so unforgivable?

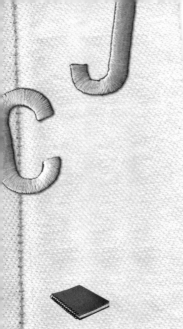

These kinds of verses can make us wonder, "Is this the fine print about God? Is this the clause at the end of the contract?" If it is, how do we sin against the Holy Spirit? Could we have already done it? If so, are we condemned already as dead people walking?

To think of something as *unforgivable* seems to go against what we like most about our relationship with God. We like the comfort and the security. We like a relationship built not on our own ability but what someone else has done on our behalf. Underneath it all, we like knowing that we can always come back. We count on it. We build our lives on it. We use it as an unshakable foundation in a world full of flux. If that foundation goes away, we are forced to live a life looking over our shoulders. Is that the fearful existence God has planned for us?

The Sabbath was established by God in order to give His people rest and remind them of His covenant with Israel, but the religious leaders turned the Sabbath blessing into a list of prohibitions. Thirty-nine tasks were banned such as tying and untying a knot! This explains Jesus' desire to break the minute, unholy restrictions of the Sabbath law.

PREVIOUSLY IN JERUSALEM ...

As always, in order to understand a verse of the Bible, we need to look at what was happening around that verse. At this moment in Jesus' ministry, everyone was confused about His identity. Some claimed Him to be the Messiah. Others wondered how He could be the Messiah, since they were looking for a military leader rather than a compassionate healer. Matthew 12 reveals conversations and questions about Jesus' identity as He healed a man's hand *on the Sabbath* and then enabled a blind and mute man to speak.

"Moving on from there, He entered their synagogue. There He saw a man who had a paralyzed hand. And in order to accuse Him they asked Him, 'Is it lawful to heal on the Sabbath?'

"But He said to them, 'What man among you, if he had a sheep that fell into a pit on the Sabbath, wouldn't take hold of it and lift it out? A man is worth far more than a sheep, so it is lawful to do good on the Sabbath.'

"Then He told the man, 'Stretch out your hand.' So he stretched it out, and it was restored, as good as the other. But the Pharisees went out and plotted against Him, how they might destroy Him" (Matthew 12:9-14).

"Then a demon-possessed man who was blind and unable to speak was brought to Him. He healed him, so that the man could both speak and see. And all the crowds were astounded and said, 'Perhaps this is the Son of David!'

"When the Pharisees heard this, they said, 'The man drives out demons only by Beelzebub, the ruler of the demons.'

"Knowing their thoughts, He told them: 'Every kingdom divided against itself is headed for destruction, and no city or house divided against itself will stand. If Satan drives out Satan, he is divided against himself. How then will his kingdom stand? And if I drive out demons by Beelzebub, who is it your sons drive them out by? For this reason they will be your judges. If I drive out demons by the Spirit of God, then the kingdom of God has come to you'" (Matthew 12:22-28).

What are some of the most popular ideas about Jesus' identity today?

What could be the source of some people's reluctance to acknowledge Jesus as God?

While studying this session, look for the most outrageous Jesus paraphernalia you can find and bring it your group meeting. Simply Google *Jesus or Jesus products* and here are a few of the unsettling things you might find: Christmas Jesus Dress up, Jesus ring tones, "Jesus Is My Homeboy" T-shirts, bobble-head dolls, talking action figure, mouse pad, various figurines, and a lamp.

Some religious leaders of the first century thought they had Jesus' identity all figured out — the scribes and Pharisees. It was clear to them who Jesus was. He healed on the Sabbath, breaking a basic staple of Jewish tradition established by God Himself. He also made preposterous claims about Himself and His own power. He didn't cast out demons with the first century methods they were familiar with: incantations and spells, potions, herbs, and magical trinkets. Jesus simply commanded the demons to leave, from His own authority, and they went.

There was only one conclusion for the Pharisees about Jesus' identity — He was a messenger of Satan. That was why He broke tradition. That was why He so easily commanded demons. And if this was true, it was a serious charge. Practicing magic under the influence of Satan was a capital offense in that society, punishable by stoning.

Jesus denied these claims, with a logical argument. It would be foolish for any army to divide it if it wanted victory. Why would He cast *out* demons if He was working *for* them? And that point is where He makes this "unforgivable" statement we are studying. He said the claims the Pharisees were making came dangerously close to a sin that God would not forgive. That sin, the rule-changing sin, the sin that can throw us into confusion and fear, is the unforgivable sin of the blasphemy of the Holy Spirit.

THE UNFORGIVABLE

We have some inkling about what the word blasphemy means, though those ideas come mostly from movies about religious zealots punishing revolutionaries. If we turn back to the Old Testament, we find that blasphemy was defined there as deliberate, defiant sin against God. The punishment, as outlined in Numbers 15:30-31, was that the violator would be cut off from his people. The Jews considered blasphemy against God to be unforgivable.

"But the person who acts defiantly, whether native or foreign resident, blasphemes the Lord. That person is to be cut off from his people. He will certainly be cut off, because he has despised the Lord's word and broken His command; his guilt remains on him" (Numbers 15:30-31).

Jesus qualified this sin even further to be a sin specifically against the Holy Spirit. Isn't it interesting that Jesus isolated this one particular form of blasphemy to the point of saying, in essence, "You can blaspheme Me if you want, but not the Holy Spirit"? The Son of God seems, in this moment when there is so much conjecture and discrepancy about His identity, to remain relatively unconcerned. He seems to be saying, "Say what you will about Me; say what you want about My Father in heaven because you can come back from those comments. But be careful — tread lightly on the issue of the Holy Spirit." That leads us to ask what this sin of blasphemy against the Spirit is, and why it is so devastating.

TRUE EXPOSURE

Maybe the answer is to be found in part by examining what exactly the Holy Spirit does here in our midst. According to John 16:8, the spirit's role is in the area of conviction:

"When He comes, He will convict the world about sin, righteousness, and judgment" (John 16:8).

Listen to "By a Thread" by Jill Phillips as you read this session.

Name some other words that mean basically the same thing as conviction. Describe the process of conviction from your own experience.

Similarly, the Holy Spirit works delicately to "expose" our sin in the presence of God's holiness. As the definition suggests, He "purposefully uncovers" our flaws in order to present us as a picture of Himself.

The meaning of *conviction* can range from blaming to shaming to investigation, but in the New Testament, the meaning seems to primarily be "expose." That is the role of the Holy Spirit. To a world that thinks it is on the right track, that greater tolerance brings greater enlightenment, and that there are no moral absolutes, the Holy Spirit steps in and exposes the error of that kind of thinking.

The Risk of Overexposure
In photography, the energy in a photon of light causes a chemical change to photographic detectors on film. Silver-halide crystals are the essence of the film because they chemically change when exposed to different degrees of light. This exposure is crucial. If film is underexposed, the crystals will not detect the reflected light from a scene, and the picture will appear too dark. If all the crystals are overexposed, the picture will appear glaringly white.

The conviction of the Holy Spirit is the reason that any of us have a Christian perspective at all. We can say that our spiritual life has come through the influence of a friend or parents or a pastor, but ultimately, we would not be spiritually alive if the Holy Spirit had not invaded our lives and convinced us of our need to repent. That is what He does — He brings life where there is death. He brings conviction where there is pride. It is through the exposure of the Holy Spirit that we repent of our sin. Without the life-giving, repentance-prompting, pride-busting influence of the Holy Spirit in our lives, we would never repent of our sins and never receive forgiveness.

What Jesus appeared to be saying was this: You can say what you want about me. You can say what you want about my Father. Evil and wicked as it may be, there is still hope for you when you do those things because the Holy Spirit can still work in your life. However, when you continually resist the truth of God exposed to you through the Holy Spirit, when you refuse to listen to Him as He convicts you about the wrongness of your world view, if you persist in considering the ways of Jesus to be foolishness, then you have shut out your opportunity for forgiveness. You have continually and willfully belittled the Spirit's work in your life.

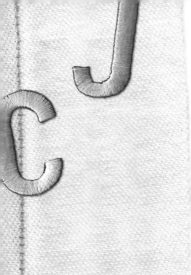

The track of the blasphemy of the Spirit looks like this: forgiveness is offered to all who repent. Those who repent do so under the influence of the Holy Spirit. If you do not accept the Spirit's voice in your life, then you will never repent. If you never repent, you will never receive forgiveness. This is the blasphemy of the Holy Spirit; it is a continual act of resistance that belittles the Spirit so grievously that He withdraws forever, rendering us unable to repent.

People who have had the Holy Spirit withdraw His influence from them are a sad case. They no longer consider Christianity as a possible lifestyle. They regard it as supremely foolish — as a crutch for the weak. They see themselves as too intellectual for children's stories and too mature for miracles. By their hardened heart and seared conscience, they bear witness to the withdrawal of the Spirit.

HOPE FOR THE UNFORGIVABLE

There is, nevertheless, a message of hope in this disconcerting teaching from Jesus. What Jesus meant as a warning to those who opposed the work of God in the world, we can actually take as great encouragement. We are not meant to look over our shoulder, constantly asking whether or not we have committed this mysterious sin.

The way we find our security is through the question itself. Those who have committed blasphemy of the Holy Spirit will not question themselves on it. Their hearts are hardened to the things of God. They don't care if they have committed this sin because they don't believe in sin or the Holy Spirit. There is security in asking the question because even the examination of ourselves is evidence of the work of the spirit in our lives. Our very concern makes a huge statement about who God is in our lives.

It is somewhat disconcerting to leave a question hanging out there without an answer, but could it be possible that this is precisely how God wants it to be? Despite living in a postmodern world, the remnants of modernism still hang over us and are intertwined in our faith. Modernism was marked by an empirical, formulaic way of thinking and processing. One result of all that is the belief that every question must have an answer and every mystery must have a solution. But perhaps God does not want all of the questions answered. Maybe leaving that sense of mystery pushes us deeper and deeper into faith.

Listen to audio file "Being a Dad." Whether you're a parent or not, you'll relate to the profound nature of the question.

How comfortable are you with mysteries in your faith? Why would He want to preserve any mystery?

Do you see how letting the question *be* the answer is the opposite of the Pharisees' attitude in this passage? They didn't want answers; they wanted to teach. They were not listeners; they were talkers. Ultimately, they were not humble; they were full of pride. Unlike them, when we let the question be the answer, it reveals much about who we are and who God is to us. It reveals a heart that is genuinely seeking.

When we ask about life, God's will, doing the best thing with our lives, and making sure we have not grieved the Spirit, we show a genuine concern for the things of God. We show that we care about those issues. Even when we don't know the answer, caring about it is perhaps the most accurate assessment of who we are — those that have faith yet still seek understanding. This is the paradox of us: We believe, and yet we have questions; we know, and yet there is mystery.

Amazingly, this is just how God wants it. What this says to the outside world is that my faith exceeds my understanding. My faith in who God is in my life is greater than my questions. I believe that His love for me is not dependent on my ability to know the right answer to every question. I believe His love for me is the starting point to a journey, not the destination.

Processing ...

☐ Break a commonly accepted rule in life this week. For example, use a fork to eat soup.

☐ Engage your community in a discussion of this question: "Does God really want us to be sure of everything?"

☐ Sit outside in silence for one hour. During that time, think about the place that "wonder" has in your life.

Notes

Notes

"I Didn't Come to Bring Peace"

Adolf Hitler. Genghis Khan. Joseph Stalin. Alexander the Great. Jesus of Nazareth.

The great Jewish Rabbi does not seem to fit in a list with these names. The other men were leaders, true, but not in the same way as Jesus. They were violent and bloodthirsty. They were power-hungry war-mongers. But Jesus — Jesus is the opposite of those men. He is peaceful and serene. He is loving and compassionate. It doesn't seem appropriate to talk about Jesus in the same breath as these tyrants.

Unless there is an element of the ministry and life of Jesus that we, understandably, neglect. Unless Jesus came to the earth for much more than peace. Unless, in some ways, Jesus is more like a general than a teacher.

"I came to bring fire on the earth, and how I wish it were already set ablaze! But I have a baptism to be baptized with, and how it consumes Me until it is finished! Do you think that I came here to give peace to the earth? No, I tell you, but rather division! From now on, five in one household will be divided: three against two, and two against three. They will be divided, father against son, son against father, mother against daughter, daughter against mother, mother-in-law against her daughter-in-law, and daughter-in-law against mother-in-law," (Luke 12:49-53).

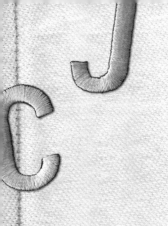

"I Didn't Come to Bring Peace"

A WAR THAT BINDS

HIS NAME IS ...

Our titles change. As time passes, our associations with people change. Therefore, the way that people refer to us changes. We move from being called brother to uncle, sister to aunt, from Robbie to Robert, Katie to Kate, from son to dad — you get the idea. Our changes in title do not affect our fundamental identity; they just express our changing relationships.

The same is true of our relationship with the Son of God. Perhaps we should call him the Lion of Judah or maybe the Great Physician or the Bread of Life or the Prince of Peace. Surely you have referred to Him in different ways during different seasons of your life depending on how you related to Him. Jesus is called by many names throughout the Old and New Testament, everything from Savior, to Brother, to King, to the Suffering Servant.

What is the one title for Jesus that has special meaning for you?

What situation in your life highlighted that particular title for you?

Invariably, we tend to see Jesus in the way that is most meaningful for us in our current situation. At times when we have been disobedient, we see Jesus as the forgiver. When we have difficult situations in our lives, we see Him as the Great Physician. Our changing association reveals a dynamic relationship. It shows that our vision of Him is growing and our faith is deepening. It's important to remember that there is the possibility that we might come upon some aspect of Jesus' identity that we feel uncomfortable with. That's how authentic relationships work. They surprise you sometimes, and you have to process through them.

JESUS THE PRINCE OF *WAR?*

The opening few minutes of Saving Private Ryan portray a graphic, overwhelming battle scene, not usually linked with images of Christ. At 6:30 a.m. on June 6, 1944, a landing craft makes its way to Omaha Beach as bullets from German guns whiz by U.S. soldiers. There is death and confusion everywhere as many abandon their boats only to be dragged down by the heavy equipment. The sound of war is unimaginable.

We do not often refer to Jesus in the context of war. In our prayers, we do not address Him as general or warrior. Maybe this is because war, though we may see it as necessary, is quite different from our vision of the Prince of Peace. And the truth is, there are many verses in the Bible that highlight the peace that comes from Jesus:

"Therefore, since we have been declared righteous by faith, we have peace with God through our Lord Jesus Christ. Also through Him, we have obtained access by faith into this grace in which we stand, and we rejoice in the hope of the glory of God" (Romans 5:1-2).

"Then I saw a new heaven and a new earth, for the first heaven and the first earth had passed away, and the sea existed no longer. I also saw the Holy City, new Jerusalem, coming down out of heaven from God, prepared like a bride adorned for her husband.

> **Then I heard a loud voice from the throne:**
> **Look! God's dwelling is with men,**
> **and He will live with them.**
> **They will be His people,**
> **and God Himself will be with them and be their God.**
> **He will wipe away every tear from their eyes.**
> **Death will exist no longer;**
> **grief, crying, and pain will exist no longer,**
> **because the previous things have passed away.**

"There's a peace only to be found on the other side of war. If that war should come I will fight it!"
— King Arthur in the "First Knight"

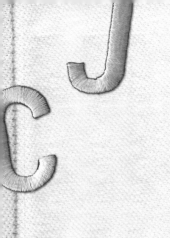

Then the One seated on the throne said, 'Look! I am making everything new.' He also said, 'Write, because these words are faithful and true'" (Revelation 21:1-5).

"For I am persuaded that neither death nor life, nor angels nor rulers, nor things present, nor things to come, nor powers, nor height, nor depth, nor any other created thing will have the power to separate us from the love of God that is in Christ Jesus our Lord!" (Romans 8:38-39).

"Don't worry about anything, but in everything, through prayer and petition with thanksgiving, let your requests be made known to God" (Philippians 4:6).

It's clear from these Scriptures that Jesus was the bringer of peace; we don't think of Him as the bringer of war. But when you consider other passages, like the ones below, you have to wonder if perhaps we have missed part of His real mission. In these passages, Jesus seems to almost thumb His nose at any kind of peaceful picture of Himself. Not only that, He seems to be explicitly saying that He did not come to bring people together, but possibly to break even the closest of human relationships.

"I came to bring fire on the earth, and how I wish it were already set ablaze! But I have a baptism to be baptized with, and how it consumes Me until it is finished! Do you think that I came here to give peace to the earth? No, I tell you, but rather division! From now on, five in one household will be divided: three against two, and two against three. They will be divided, father against son, son against father, mother against daughter, daughter against mother, mother-in-law against her daughter-in-law, and daughter-in-law against mother-in-law" (Luke 12:49-53).

"Don't assume that I came to bring peace on the earth. I did not come to bring peace, but a sword. For I came to turn a man against his father, a daughter against her mother, a daughter-in-law against her mother-in-law; and a man's enemies will be the members of his household.

"The person who loves father or mother more than Me is not worthy of Me; the person who loves son or daughter more than Me is not worthy of Me. And whoever doesn't take up his cross and follow Me is not worthy of Me. Anyone finding his life will lose it, and anyone losing his life because of Me will find it" (Matthew 10:34-39).

What emotions do these passages evoke in you?

How does the cost of following Christ described in these passages reflect what you have experienced?

How do you reconcile the two views of Jesus — peace-giver and conflict-starter?

PUT YOURSELF IN *THEIR* SHOES

In order to understand how Jesus words would have hit the listening crowd, keep in mind three things. First, at this point in His ministry, Jesus was speaking to a predominantly Jewish audience. It wasn't until the accounts of the early church in Acts, after Jesus' death, resurrection and ascension back to God, that the gospel spread officially beyond the Jewish culture. At that time, these first Jewish believers, led by the apostles, made the huge realization that the gospel was not for Jews alone. Coming to grips with that single decision required apostolic dreams, miracles, conflicts and a now-famous leadership council.

Next, we need to understand that Jesus' words about family would have been particularly tough for this Jewish audience. The Jews existed in a culture built on family and tradition. People did not change classes or lifestyles; a fisherman was born into a fisherman's family, lived a fisherman's life, and died a fisherman after having raised fisher-children. Divorce was a life-and-death matter, and the community shunned those who broke that bond.

Family Ties
God placed supreme importance on the family in both the Old and New Testaments. In fact, half of the Old Testament capital crimes were family-related. In the New Testament, family structures also included all extended family members. Roles were generally outlined by Jesus and Paul.

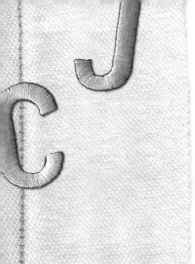

Finally, remember that as much as these people believed in family, their whole belief system was categorically based on the existence of only one God. Anyone who claimed equality with God was considered a blasphemer, also punishable by death. This is why Jesus' message and presence were so divisive. To first century Jewish ears, He was the worst of heretics, offensive to the very core of their history and their identity. (That is, unless what He was saying was true. Then He was actually their Savior.)

So understanding the audience and the culture of the time, you can see that Jesus' words about division were quite appropriate. For Him to walk into that culture and say, "I and my heavenly Father are One," (gasp!) and then begin to gather a contingent of those who believed Him, there is no way that conflict would not ensue — and yes, family member against family member. He was instigating a transition, a shift in spiritual understanding that we haven't seen the end of yet.

His warnings were already taking place. Look at the first disciples. They actually left their nets to follow Christ. Those nets were more than just something they were doing — they were the family business. They were their heritage. They were their source of income and identity. They abandoned it for the unknown. In doing that, they put the relationships they'd built in their previous life in serious jeopardy.

What has faith cost you in terms of relationships? Including both family and friends? What about co-workers?

CONFLICTED MISSION?

We think about these kinds of things to figure out how conflict fits within Jesus' mission. Most of us would say that verses like John 3:16-17 describe Jesus' mission:

"'For God loved the world in this way: He gave His One and Only Son, so that everyone who believes in Him will not perish but have eternal life. For God did not send His Son into the world that He might judge the world, but that the world might be saved through Him" (John 3:16-17).

> In your own words, what was Jesus' mission all about?
> As people joined in with Jesus, what changes happened in their lives?

Jesus did come to bring peace between God and mankind. His was not a mission of condemnation but of salvation. This is the mission that we have joined and even offer to others. It is the mission that motivated Jesus to cry over Jerusalem. It is this mission that He commanded His disciples to adopt as their life creed.

Without this, all of mankind would be at war with God, whether aware of it or not. Without it, we would walk through life without true purpose, lost in the tangle of our own selfishness and desires. Because of it, however, we can live in a constant state of rest with God, knowing that we have nothing left to prove to Him because Jesus has been righteous and good on our behalf. Because of that mission, we can live in the security of being God's sons and daughters. Jesus paid the debt that had kept humanity at odds with its creator.

Perhaps the way the ideas of peace and conflict can coexist in the person of Jesus is by understanding that there is a difference between His mission and *the effect* of His mission.

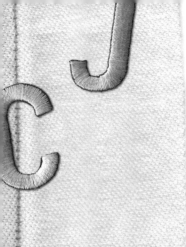

As comforting as that mission of salvation and reconciliation continues to be, there is an uncomfortable effect associated with it even today — 20-plus centuries after Jesus' words were spoken. Making this peace with God can still bring about a kind of war in our lives. We should not be surprised about this effect. Jesus was very clear about it, and we've seen it on a practical level throughout history:

- Martin Luther King, Jr. wanted to preach a message of peace and equality, but an act of violence ended his life.
- Ghandi, who promoted non-violence and peace throughout his life, was killed by an assassin's bullet at the age of 79.
- John Lennon who wrote the words, "give peace a chance" was killed with a gunshot.

> **Why should it be any different for Jesus who is the ultimate peace bringer?**

Violence can be a by-product of someone's attempt to bring about peace. Jesus was clear that the peace He was bringing to the earth involved such a radical internal change in people's lives that it would put them at odds with the world around them.

But it can still be a bit puzzling for us today. As we come to faith in Christ, our lives change. The Spirit indwells us. His fruit should become obvious: love, joy, peace, patience, kindness, goodness, gentleness meekness, self-control. So while we can understand more of the conflict of the first century believers, today when the gospel is for all people and Jesus' message is familiar in many cultures — why would it still bring about conflict?

> **When you first came to faith, was there a "prying loose" with any of your family or friends? Who? Why?**

NEW VANTAGE POINT

People who make a change into a life that presses hard into God can find themselves at odds with the people they have been close to. Actually, any new allegiance can do that to a certain extent (new boyfriend, new job …). When the change is such a deeply spiritual one, though, people can even find themselves at war with their culture in general. It's the *effect* of a new life in Jesus with its inherent new choices and altered world view.

That doesn't mean that Jesus sets out to make you an enemy of the state. What it does mean is that as His child, you will look at the world from a whole new vantage point. Forging a relationship with God Himself changes the way you relate to the world.

You also have a new sense of confidence. You belong in a new way to someone who loves you unconditionally. You're full of a sense of mission. Your eyes are opened to the way you want to influence, to the way you want to change your life and frame your belief system. You've stepped into a love relationship that makes you different.

Simply put, sometimes, once you step into faith, you feel more freedom to take on more battles. When you enter the state of peace with God because of Christ, there's security waiting. God is not going to "break up" with His children. You are secure. That brings confidence. Sometimes that confidence allows you to declare all-out war on the things you see around you that work against God's purposes.

Listen to the audio file "The 'God' Card" and learn about the one move that actually trumps it. Then think about this: What relationship in your life is totally secure?

DESTINATION DETERMINED

The fight the new life in Christ prompts is not just about sin; it is also about circumstances. Peace with God gives you the security to look your life circumstances in the eye and beat them back with faith. In Luke 12:50, Jesus spoke passionately about His mission. He was distressed until it was accomplished. As we connect with Jesus, we connect with that mission. Just as anything that we feel passionately about, it stirs us up, it distresses us. When we are that filled with a sense of purpose, we are less likely to be caught up in every wind of circumstance that blows. We are more likely to act upon life, rather than react to it.

> What courage does your relationship with God offer you in facing life?

How does this courage relate to the conflict that Jesus' truth brought into the lives of His followers?

THE BIGGEST LOSER WINS

Walking in the way of Jesus can also cause friction within us. What do you do with the seemingly irreconcilable truth that this life of conflict Jesus seems to be offering does not seem like the abundant one He describes in John 10:10?

"A thief comes only to steal and to kill and to destroy. I have come that they may have life and have it in abundance" (John 10:10).

This verse can inspire hope because we take it to mean that life with Jesus is better. You gain something you did not have before. Right? *Right?* But let's compare that passage with Jesus' words in Matthew 10:38-39. He says if you don't lose your life, you won't find it. He talked about taking up your cross — a tool of execution. Reading that, it can seem like life with Jesus is not about gain at all; it's more about loss.

Let's look more closely. Jesus says that if you don't take up your cross and follow Him, then you can't follow Him at all. He goes one step further in a parallel passage in Luke 9:23, saying that you must take up your cross daily and follow Him.

"Then He said to [them] all, 'If anyone wants to come with Me, he must deny himself, take up his cross daily, and follow Me'" (Luke 9:23).

If that sounds strange to us, then it would have sounded unthinkably strange to the people He was talking to. Here was a band of His followers He was sending out on a mission to do great things; they were chomping at the bit to get started. It was time for a pep rally, the final hurrah. And right then, Jesus begins this bit about losing your life. What a downer. Maybe they were able to understand the part about leaving their father and mother and children. After all, they had all done that already. They had left a great deal to follow Him.

But when He brought in the cross, it must have caught them off-guard. This is not language about simply leaving something behind; this is language about death. It's language about being punished for doing something wrong rather than being rewarded for doing something right. In essence, He says, "I know you think I am stretching it, but I'm not. This mission is going to cost you everything."

> In your own words, in what ways does the Christian life involve loss?

DYING TO LIVE

It's easier to think about what we gain as Christians rather than what we lose, isn't it? It's easier to think about the abundance part of Jesus' mission than the sacrifice part. It's easier to deal with the Prince of Peace than the prophetic warrior portrayed in Matthew 10 and Luke 12.

There's a familiar knot that forms in our stomachs when we are faced with the sacrifices we make in following Christ: Lose your self-sufficiency, lose your destructive habits, and maybe lose your girlfriend. Lose your freedom to do anything you want any time you want, lose your attitude, lose your hate for your enemies, lose your vengeance, lose your potty mouth. Jesus was clear: If you want to walk with Him, you have to be prepared to go against the flow.

So how do we bring together both concepts in the teachings of Christ — abundance and sacrifice? Peace and conflict?

The truth is, a Christian theology that is built around only one or the other is not a complete theology. These concepts both go together. Jesus is not saying that He wants you to lose your life — end of story. He is saying that He wants you to find your life, but loss will be part of the process. He comes to bring new life, but to enter a new life, you have to let go of your old one.

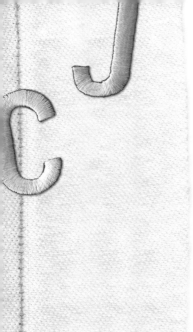

How can losing be the way to go about gaining?

As a Christian, what do you gain and what do you lose because of your faith?

Listen to "Lost at Sea" by Jimmy Needham. In what areas of your life do you feel lost?

ONE FINAL THOUGHT

Jesus described the life of faith as a life that brings you peace, which can, in turn, bring you conflict. Perhaps in this passage filled with war images, there's one more thing for us to consider. Have you ever considered just how much of your life you spend trying to prove yourself to other people? Have you thought about how much energy you put into pleasing others, or trying to feel OK with the fact that you haven't?

Jesus' words to His followers were all about losing the value that they associated with their attachments — even their families. Perhaps within His message to that audience — an even more family-driven culture than our own — there is a specific message for us. Jesus has called us to a higher purpose than to simply drift through life validating ourselves by any one set of relationships.

How do we have close friendships, but still find our ultimate validation from God?

Jesus has called us to lose your lives — to live separate from all attachments — and therefore to find real life. Through finding life in Him, we have the chance to reclaim the whole reason we were put here in the first place. We have the chance, by stepping away from all of the typical things that validate our existence, to hear the voice of the Holy Spirit at last telling us who we are to God. We have the chance to live a life built around the important things in the universe. It is an incredible offer, not of loss, but of gain. It is the offer to face conflicts, and maybe even to prompt some, but to have the Prince of Peace in the midst of it all.

Processing ...

☐ Engage someone in a conversation that has differing opinions about the war than you do. Mostly listen.

☐ Consider this: What is the most uncomfortable title of Jesus? Journal about why that perspective is troubling to you.

☐ Plan a viewing of "Saving Private Ryan" with your small group.

Notes

Notes

Notes

Notes

GROUP CONTACT INFORMATION

Name _____ Number _____
Email _____

Name _____ Number _____
Email _____

Name _____ Number _____
Email _____

Name _____ Number _____
Email _____

Name _____ Number _____
Email _____

Name _____ Number _____
Email _____

Name _____ Number _____
Email _____

Name _____ Number _____
Email _____

Name _____ Number _____
Email _____

Name _____ Number _____
Email _____

Name _____ Number _____
Email _____

Name _____ Number _____
Email _____

Name _____ Number _____
Email _____

Name _____ Number _____
Email _____

Name _____ Number _____
Email _____

Name _____ Number _____
Email _____

Name _____ Number _____
Email _____

Name _____ Number _____
Email _____

Name _____ Number _____
Email _____

Name _____ Number _____
Email _____

What is Threads?

WE ARE A COMMUNITY OF PEOPLE WHO ARE PIECING THE CHRISTIAN LIFE TOGETHER, ONE EXPERIENCE AT A TIME.

We're rooted in Romans 12 and Colossians 3. We're serious about worshipping God with our lives. We want to understand the grace Jesus extended to us on the cross and act on it. We want community, need to worship, and aren't willing to sit on our hands when the world needs help. We want to grow. We crave Bible study that raises questions, makes us think, and causes us to own our faith. We're interested in friendships that are as strong as family ties — the kind of relationships that transform individuals into communities.

Our Bible studies are designed specifically for you, featuring flexible formats with engaging video, audio, and music. These discussion-driven studies intentionally foster group and individual connections and encourage practical application of Scripture.

   You'll find topical articles, staff and author blogs, podcasts, and lots of other great resources at:

THREADSMEDIA.COM

STOP BY TO JOIN OUR ONLINE COMMUNITY AND COME BY TO VISIT OFTEN!

INTRANSIT: WHAT DO YOU DO WITH YOUR WAIT?
by Mike Harder

Do you often feel that you're waiting for real life to begin? This study introduces you to three truths about waiting as it traces the lives of David, Jesus, and Joseph — all promised great things and all of whom waited, sometimes painfully, to see God's promises come to pass. You'll discover that waiting without purpose can lead to loneliness and doubting God, but purposeful waiting brings a sense of fulfillment and an awareness of God's timing and faithfulness.

Mike Harder is a regular face and speaker at The Loop in Memphis, Tenn., a weekly Bible study for young adults. He also serves on the staff of Highpoint Church overseeing the church's connection ministry.

THE EXCHANGE:
TIRED OF LIVING THE CHRISTIAN LIFE ON YOUR OWN?
by Joel Engle

And exploration of Romans 6, 7, and 8, this study helps you understand that the power of the Christian life is found not in yourself or religious activity, but in "exchanging" your life for the life of Jesus Christ. You'll learn how to overcome sin and personal hang-ups through a life of dependency on Christ.

Joel Engle is a worship communicator who uses his gifts to impact lives and glorify God. In The Exchange, Joel shares his own story of finally understanding what the Christian life is all about and learning to depend solely on Christ.

GET UNCOMFORTABLE:
SERVE THE POOR. STOP INJUSTICE.
CHANGE THE WORLD ... IN JESUS' NAME
by Todd Phillips

Phillips guides you to understand how your faith in Christ and concern for the poor go hand-in-hand. As he examines God's character and perspective regarding poverty and injustice, he offers an understanding of what God calls you to do, along with practical ways to impact culture by caring for "the least of these."

Todd Phillips is the teaching pastor of Frontline, the young adult ministry of McLean Bible Church near Washington D.C. His passions are teaching the people of God and sharing the Gospel with those who aren't yet Christians. He is the author of CPR: Reviving a Flat-lined Generation.

For full details on all of Threads' studies,
visit www.threadsmedia.com.

IN TRANSIT →

WHAT DO YOU DO WITH YOUR WAIT?

MIKE HARDER

Table of Contents
INTRANSIT: WHAT DO YOU DO WITH YOUR WAIT?

Meet the Author

MIKE HARDER

My name is Mike Harder, and I'm pretty much a normal guy who enjoys coffee (*lots* of coffee), wakeboarding, and several other sports. To know anything about me, you have to know the context of my life: I'm a missionary kid from Bogota, Colombia, where my parents served for 28 years as church planters. Colombia is an incredible country, but it's troubled politically and socially due to civil war, drug trafficking, and terrorism that have plagued it for the past 40 years. I love being from Colombia, but God has called me to work in the United States as my mission field. I graduated from Mid-America Baptist Theological Seminary in Memphis, Tenn., with a Master of Divinity and am now on staff at Highpoint Church as a speaker guy for The Loop, a large single adult Bible study, as well as director of our church's connection ministry. I am truly motivated by the opportunity to make an impact in the spiritual health and condition of the people in my generation. Thanks for taking time out to learn how to wait well. Come by and visit me at *www.mikeharderministries.com*.

0017

Welcome to InTransit
A TRIP IN DISCOVERING HOW TO MAKE THE MOST OF YOUR WAIT

Whether grounded at the airport or standing in the never-ending line at the DMV, we're familiar with the waiting game.

We may not like it, but it's something we do. For most of our lives, we've been waiting for something — a driver's license, a graduation, a birthday, a spouse, a job … And from here until Eternity, we'll be waiting for whatever's next.

Author Mike Harder is a professional "waiter." He's logged countless hours at the airport on mission trips. He's stood in eternally long lines for that perfect cup of coffee. He's waited on God to bring the right job, right group of friends, and right girl. And he waited for God to give him new purpose after realizing that the plans he had for his life, while good, were not the plans God had in mind.

InTransit: What Do You Do with Your Wait? traces the lives of a few of the Bible's most influential men — Joseph, David, and Jesus — who were promised great things concerning their lives and waited, sometimes painfully, to see God's promises come to pass. What was true for them remains true for you today: There is great purpose in the waiting.

Like any great journey in life, you don't want to wait alone — and you don't want to go through this study alone. So grab some friends, wrangle a leader from your church, and figure out a consistent time to meet together to talk, process, and pray about what you're learning.

Here's a great tip: read the session you're going to talk about before you get together with your group; that way, you'll be better prepared to inject your ideas into the discussion. Others will be counting on hearing your insight, wisdom, and experiences as well as what you're hearing from God.

At the end of each session, you'll see a section called "In the Meantime …" The ideas listed there can help you connect with and process what you're reading. So, take advantage of those every chance you get before your group meeting. Finally, there are some really cool pages for journaling in the back of this book. We've provided those because we believe you're going to have a lot to think about and say to God — and yourself — throughout this study. So you don't forget any of the good (and, OK, possibly difficult) stuff, write it down, draw it out, whatever you need to do process what you're discovering about yourself and your wait. (Check out the article on the follow pages for ideas to get started on your journal.)

Thanks for joining us — it's going to be an exciting wait!

In The Waiting Room

In the spring of 2005, having seen the effects of the tsunami that rocked Southeast Asia, our church commissioned me to lead a team that would provide aid to a very remote and affected area on the island of Sumatra. We had an incredible time of service (minus the modern comforts of air conditioning, hot water, and walls). But when it was time to go home, we hit a roadblock.

In most emerging countries, air transportation to rural areas is sketchy, at best. Due to the damage to the country's infrastructure, we were told that getting a flight back would be hit or miss.

Minutes soon turned into hours and frustrations started to mount in the 100-degree heat. Slowly melting into a puddle of sticky goo, I got an epiphany: *I really hate waiting!*

Now I have always been somewhat driven and impatient, but my loathing for *having to wait* grew to new dimensions. In the soup of delirious thoughts floating through my head, I wondered why waiting is such a terrible thing.

Have you ever been stuck somewhere that left you incredibly frustrated? The duration of your wait may have caused emotions to simmer to the surface. I personally feel like I have been waiting my entire life for stuff; silly stuff, like the doctor (even when I arrived on time), or the bathroom when my sister was taking forever , or for much more serious stuff like the right job, getting things right with a friend, or the right person to marry.

I believe that, regardless of where we are in life, we are all waiting for something — for whatever is next. This can be a major issue, a gaping hole in our lives, in our "happiness quest" that gnaws at us like a scavenging rodent chewing on some Limburger.

Some of you have been waiting a long time for your issue or situation to be resolved, others for a much shorter time, but all of you are asking the same questions: *What should I be doing differently? When is this going to end? Did I totally miss my chance? Why is this happening to me? Is there some kind of sin or shortcoming in my life that is keeping me from achieving happiness or the thing I desire most?*

In the Waiting Room
YOU ARE NOT ALONE

Be assured you are not alone; we are all waiting for what is next in our lives. The *what* may be different for you than it is for your roommate or best friend or coworker or the others in your group. Having other people to walk through the wait with you is extremely important.

As you go through this study, ask God to build and strengthen the relationships within your group. Ask Him also to open your heart and mind to the truth He wants to reveal to you during this experience. As these things register, jot down what you are thinking, feeling, and learning in the journal at the back of this book (it starts after Session 6). Refer to it often and ask God for wisdom on how to deal with the stuff He's revealing to you. And don't forget to share what He's telling you with others in your group. They will be a source of great encouragement to you. Remember: you are not alone!

Just to get started, try answering the questions in the space below.

> Write down three things you are waiting for right now. Next to each, note how long you've been waiting for them to be resolved:

Watch "Bus Stop" during your first study group session. Which character do you relate to most?

> Share two of these with your group as you are comfortable. If it's too personal, don't worry about sharing. Just record them in your journal.

TIME IS WASTING AWAY

Because waiting is extremely taxing, it's hard to avoid thinking about the issues for which we desire true resolution. We numb ourselves to our own realities by over scheduling our lives; then, we're so busy doing things, we don't have any time to dwell on what is frustrating us.

Maybe you end up watching a lot of television or just hang out by yourself at a coffee shop. As a result you avoid meeting new people. Or, you may go the opposite direction and try to solve things yourself, tackling every situation with total independence.

Every once in a while, however, a moment of silence sneaks in and we are faced with reality and all the emotional frustration and loneliness that a wait often brings — and then, the questions rush in.

I know that you try to escape and numb out of stuff in your life; I know because I do it, too. In fact, sometimes it can be fun to numb out — but it's not healthy. The first way to get past this is to come face-to-face with what you're doing and why.

> def·i·ni·tion
> /num/
> **to make incapable of action or of feeling emotion; lacking or deficient in emotion or feeling; indifferent.**

List two or three ways that you numb out. Go ahead — elaborate:

Why do you think that you look for escape?

Share one of your 'numb-out techniques' with the group.

HERE'S THE TRUTH(S)

Bummed out yet? Don't worry, there is good news! First of all, you aren't the first to go through this situation, so you're in great company. There are many godly people, from biblical times to the here-and-now, who have had to wait a long time to see their hopes and dreams come true — so there is no shame in waiting.

Second, there is purpose behind your wait and there is a way to wait with hope. Believe it or not, there is a way to be a proactive waiter. In fact, three great truths about waiting were modeled in the lives of David, Joseph, and Jesus as they followed their life missions:

Truth 1: The waiting can't be about the wait.

Truth 2: You can't short-circuit the wait.

Truth 3: God builds into you during the wait.

Over the next three sessions, we'll process these truths together. But for now, we're going to meet some guys from the Bible who waited well. We'll be learning a lot about them and how God used them — and their waits — in really significant ways.

CHARACTER STUDY

Now depending on how knowledgeable you are about the Bible, you may be familiar with these guys, or you may not know them very well at all. So here's a brief rundown. If you want to learn more, check out the sidebars on the pages of this book to learn more about them and the time in which they lived.

David was a king in Israel about 1000 B.C. He is widely regarded as being the greatest king ever in the history of Israel. He's famous in current history because he is credited with writing many of the Psalms. He's also a popular guy with children because of his battle with the giant warrior Goliath.

But David had a huge wait in his life. He was promised the kingdom when he was a young man at the age of 13 and had to wait 17 years before he received the crown. There were lots of obstacles that he had to face, and through those he learned how to trust God.

Joseph lived about 500 years earlier than David, and had to face many overwhelming odds to find success in life. Yet he managed to keep his integrity and his relationship with God intact. He had several opportunities

def·i·ni·tion
/säm/

a well-known book in the Old Testament made up of 150 songs, poems, and prayers; the word "psalms" comes from a Greek word that referred to songs that were accompanied by stringed instruments.

to take advantage of situations that he probably could have gotten away with, but Joseph submitted to God's will and timing instead. He is also well-known for his coat of many colors and eventually served as counselor to the Pharaoh of Egypt.

The third person we'll examine is the most well-known and controversial person who has ever lived; in fact, more has probably been written about Jesus than anyone else. Although Jesus was fully God, as a human, He still faced a wait. He had an incredibly urgent mission — to save the world from sin and death — but waited until the right time to bring it about.

David and Joseph may seem larger than life, fortified with character and abilities you think you could never achieve, but as you study them, take comfort in knowing that they struggled as they waited on God (often for long periods of time) to see their hopes fulfilled. Jesus faced rejection and temptation — things you've undoubtedly faced yourself.

It's my sincere desire that this study provides hope for your future and a very doable plan of action in the now despite your periods of waiting. To make it through, however, you need to harness the power of faith. Now you probably think you understand faith pretty well, but often it's a little more difficult to really grasp than we like to admit.

My friend Andy says that the distance between a promise and its completion is faith. That makes sense to me, because I have seen huge distances between promises and their fulfillment in my own life. I have discovered that sometimes I just have to trust in the plan that God has for me — but that can be really difficult to actually do.

> What do you think about having to trust God with your desires and goals for the future?

"Now faith is being sure of what we hope for and certain of what we do not see" (Hebrews 11:1-3).

Through the next five sessions, I pray that you will gain confidence that you can trust this unseen God with your wait and that He is certain and true — not something that is elusive or untrustworthy.

What would your life look like if you waited differently than you have been?

Download the *InTransit* playlist. Get the list from your group leader or at *www.threadsmedia. com/media*. Make it your "soundtrack" for this study.

It's Not Terminal
The movie *The Terminal* exemplifies the agony of waiting. The story's protagonist (Tom Hanks) travels to America to fulfill a promise made to his father. While he is in the air, his country's government is overthrown, stranding him in an airport. Despite the sudden halt of his plans, Viktor determines to keep his promise. It's an inspiring, yet quirky film you just might all be able to identify with.

PANIC ROOM?

I remember as a kid having to wait for my mom in the car when she went into a store to grab an item quickly. Even as a 10-year-old, I had developed a healthy aversion to shopping, and it was more fun to mess around with the radio and listen to music that Mom didn't think was appropriate. Usually, at some point while I was rocking out to Madonna, Guns N' Roses, or the Beach Boys (I was real hard core in back in the day!), I would forget what Mom looked like that day — what was most distinguishable about her from a distance or the way she had dressed that day.

My imagination would play tricks on me as panic started to set in; weird questions would surface, like: *Maybe she left me? Maybe she forgot where she parked?* Just when I was about to crack, she would appear, cruising effortlessly through the crowded parking lot to save the day. Relief would settle in, and the world felt OK again.

In the same way, many of us panic when we have to wait for a long period of time for the things we expect to happen in life. We tend to forget what God looks like — not what we have been taught about Him in Sunday School — but rather, what it's like to relate to Him, to feel Him near. Panic then rises in our lives like a flood of despair.

What can help you *not* forget who God is and what He looks like? That's a really tough question. The following are a few things that I think might help. Be forewarned; these aren't quick fixes or magical solutions. You won't be able to figure all this out in one sitting.

Identify one barrier in your life that might keep you from recognizing God's presence. Being aware of how it impacts your life allows you to actively and intentionally do something about it.

Recall a specific time God showed Himself faithful through one of your past experiences in life. Discuss and process that memory with a friend in your group. Share what was most painful about that time and also what was most hopeful when resolution came. (If you don't feel like that's happened in your life, ask a friend to share one of their experiences with you. Take note about what you can learn about God and your relationship with Him from that friend.)

Pray for God to move in you. That might seem like kind of a freaky prayer to pray, but do it anyway. Ask God to show up in a powerful way or draw you out of the numbness of life. Remember the words of 1 John 4:13-15.

"We know that we live in God and he lives in us, because he gave us his Spirit" (1 John 4:13).

 ## IN THE MEANTIME ...

☐ Take some time to write out a prayer about your wait. You can use the journal in the back of this book or whatever's handy (even Starbucks napkins have been known to suffice). As you write, ask God to walk through this study with you. You can't do it without Him. Pray specifically for patience and hope as you face your current wait. (Check out the article on pages 10-11 for tips on journaling your thoughts and prayers.)

☐ Encourage one person in your group this week who you know is really struggling with waiting. Send an email, actually write a personal note, or make a phone call.

In the Meantime ...

"In the Meantimes" are helpful ideas for processing what God is teaching you through this study as you spend time alone with Him. They also provide ways to connect with the study and your group between meetings.

nt suppression of those who use—an
ational rights will, in the end, only inc
re disorder and more conflict. It was.

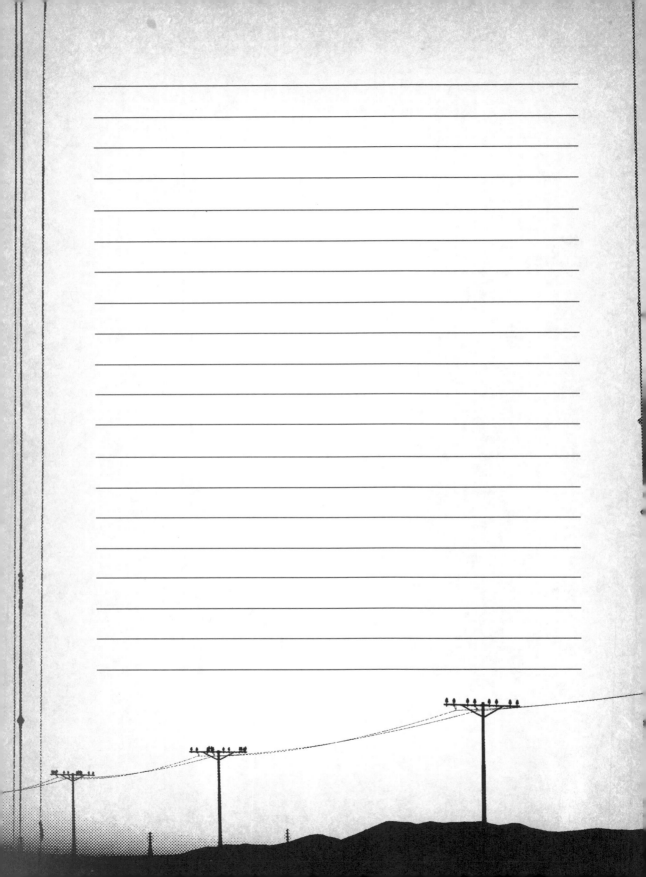

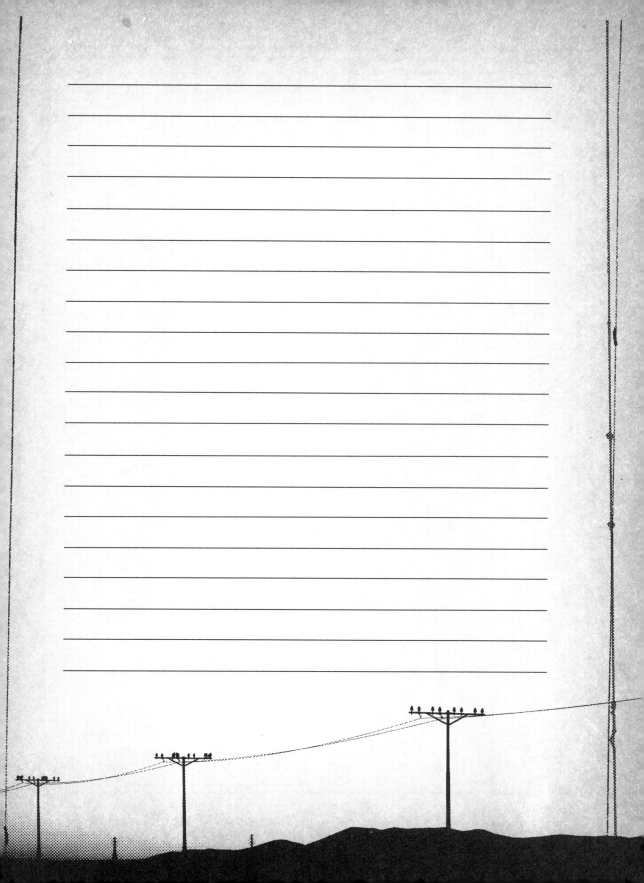